Shaken Not Stirred!

{ A Boozy Quiz }

In memory of Jim Baker, the best of drinking companions.

Compiled by Graham Tarrant

Shaken Not Stirred!

§ A Boozy Quiz §

First published in Great Britain in 2013
by Absolute Press,
an imprint of Bloomsbury Publishing Plc

Absolute Press
Scarborough House
29 James Street West
Bath BA1 2BT
Phone 44 (0) 1225 316013
Fax 44 (0) 1225 445836
E-mail office@absolutepress.co.uk
Website www.absolutepress.co.uk

Publisher Jon Croft
Commissioning Editor Meg Avent
Art Direction Matt Inwood
Design Claire Siggery
Project Editor Alice Gibbs

A catalogue record of this book is
available from the British Library.

ISBN **9781472903631**

Printed and bound in China.

A note about the text
This book was set using the fonts
Century, Rosewood and Engravers MT.
The first Century typeface was cut in
1894. In 1975 an updated family of Century
typefaces was designed by Tony Stan for
ITC. Rosewood is an ornamental font
designed in 1994 by Kim Buker Chansler,
Carl Crossgrove and Carol Twombly.
Engravers MT was created by Robert
Wiebking in 1899.

Bloomsbury Publishing Plc
50 Bedford Square, London WC1B 3DP
www.bloomsbury.com

CONTENTS

⤜⤛

AN INTRODUCTION

For some, the only drink-related question worth asking is, 'Whose round is it?' More thoughtful imbibers though have an interest in the subject that goes deeper than the bottom of their glass. After all, many of us put in long hours of research at home or at our favourite watering hole, or further afield on wine-tasting trips, distillery tours, at beer fests and the like. Chasing a saucy young wine around the palate, unpicking the 'nose' of an unfamiliar malt or tapping into the CAMRAderie of the true beer enthusiast is all part of the liquorice learning curve.

This book is a chance to put that knowledge, so diligently acquired by the dedicated drinker, to the test. The 500 alcohol-induced questions are divided into fifty themed sections that, like a well-stocked bar, cater for all tastes. One round follows another, as they are apt to do, with a few quizzical detours along the way. The connoisseur and casual drinker are equally well served.

Quizzing, like drinking, is best done in company. So get together with some kindred spirits, top up the glasses and start asking questions.

UNCORKING

THE FIZZ

1. Which Champagne owes its name to a widow?

2. Most Champagne is a blend of which three grapes?

3. Dom Pérignon is an illustrious product of which Champagne house?

4. Which Champagne bottle is larger, Balthazar or Salmanazar?

5. What is the definition of a 'vintage' Champagne?

6. Why do Champagne corks have a metal cap?

7. What is removed from the wine in the dégorgement stage of production?

8. Pol Roger produces a Champagne named after which famous Englishman?

9. White Champagne made entirely from black grapes is called what?

10. How many times is Champagne fermented?

---

1. Veuve Clicquot. Madame Clicquot, a widow (veuve), popularised her Champagne among Europe's elite in the early 19th century. 2. Chardonnay, Pinot Noir and Pinot Meunier. 3. Moet & Chandon. 4. Balthazar (equivalent to 16 standard bottles; a Salmanazar is 12). 5. Champagne made with grapes from a single vintage, supposedly only in the best years. 6. To prevent the wire muzzle cutting into the cork. 7. Sediment that has gathered in the neck of the tilted bottle. 8. Sir Winston Churchill, a voracious consumer of Pol Roger. 9. Blanc de noirs. 10. Twice.

In which language would you be saying 'Cheers!'?

1. Salud
2. Proost
3. Iechyd da
4. Chok dee
5. Prost
6. Kippis
7. Na zdravi
8. Cin cin
9. Sei gesund
10. Oogy wawa

A WEE
DRAM

1. The word whisky comes from the Gaelic *uisge beatha*, meaning what?

2. Which Scottish glen was famous for its whisky smugglers?

3. Whisky until it fully matures is called what?

4. Who were commonly known as 'gaugers'?

5. Does a vatted malt contain any grain whisky?

6. Scotland exports what percentage of its whisky: 70%, 80% or 90%?

7. What day job did poet and whisky celebrant Robert Burns undertake in 1789?

8. When did the first commercial blended whisky go on sale: 1833, 1853 or 1873?

9. What is the legal minimum amount of time Scotch must age in the cask?

10. Which major Scotch whisky brand is based in Dumbarton?

1. Water of life. 2. Glenlivet. At one time there were more than 200 illicit stills in the glen. 3. Spirit.
4. Excise officers. 5. No. It is an all-malt whisky blended from several distilleries. 6. 90 per cent.
7. He became an excise officer. 8. 1853. 9. Three years. 10. Ballantine's

1. What is Homer Simpson's beer of choice?

2. Whose friendship floated on Bolli Stoli?

3. What is Hercule Poirot's favourite liqueur?

4. Whose exotic beverages include a Caribbean Stallion?

5. What hard-drinking TV detective claimed
that 'beer is food'?

6. In *Frasier*, what is Martin Crane's preferred brand of beer?

7. Which character in *Mad Men* favours a three-Martini diet
when entertaining clients?

8. In *Sex and the City*, Carrie often settles for a Cosmopolitan
cocktail – what are the four ingredients?

9. What is the imported liquor of choice in the Prohibition-era
Boardwalk Empire?

10. Which TV medic likes to relax with an Appletini?

1. Duff Beer. **2.** Eddy's and Patsy's in Absolutely Fabulous (Bollinger champagne and Stolichnaya vodka).
3. Crème de Menthe. **4.** Del Boy's in Only Fools and Horses. **5.** Inspector Morse. **6.** Ballantine. **7.** Roger Sterling.
8. Vodka, orange liqueur, cranberry juice, freshly squeezed lime juice. **9.** Canadian Club whisky.
10. JD (Dr John Dorian) in Scrubs.

AS SEEN ON TV

BEERS
ALL ROUND

1. Which beer did British entrepreneur Karan Bilimoria launch in 1989?

2. What is the second largest market for Guinness after the UK: Ireland, Nigeria or the USA?

3. Which brand of beer called itself the 'Cream of Manchester'?

4. In what year was beer first sold in cans: 1935, 1945 or 1955?

5. Which brewer no longer rolls out the red barrel?

6. Which Welsh beer has a distinctly spiritual flavour?

7. Which brewer sponsored the England cricket team in the 1990s?

8. Where is the seaside home of Adnams beer?

9. What nation downs the most beer: China, Germany or the USA?

10. Which trademark was the first to be registered in the UK: the Bass red triangle, Courage cockerel or William Younger's 'Father William'?

1. What is red wine from Bordeaux traditionally called in the UK?

2. In what month of the year does Beaujolais Nouveau make its annual appearance?

3. Which wine commemorates the papacy's temporary shift to Avignon in the 14th century?

4. Which grape is used to make the finest red Burgundies?

5. What feature of the terrain makes the wines of the Haut-Médoc in Bordeaux so exceptional?

6. Fitou is a popular wine from which region?

7. Which one of these wines is not a Beaujolais: Brouilly, Fleurie, Givry?

8. Which wine from the Lot region is noted for its particularly dark red colour?

9. Château Cheval-Blanc is one of the premier wines of which Bordeaux area?

10. Which town is called the 'wine capital of Burgundy' and is known mainly for its reds?

1. Claret. 2. November. 3. Châteauneuf-du-Pape ('the pope's new castle'). 4. Pinot Noir. 5. The extensive gravel banks that provide perfect drainage and ripening conditions for the grapes. 6. Languedoc-Roussillon. 7. Givry is a Burgundy. 8. Cahors. 9. St-Émilion. 10. Beaune.

VIN
ROUGE

COMING
TO TERMS
WITH WHISKY

1. A whisky's aroma is known as its what?
2. What is draff?
3. Whisky is stored in a bonded warehouse until
what takes place?
4. What is the two-handled Celtic drinking vessel
ceremoniously used for whisky?
5. New make spirit, straight from the still, is also called what?
6. The practice of giving distillery employees a spirited drink
or two during the working day was known as what?
7. What word is used to describe the lingering flavour of
a whisky once it has been swallowed?
8. What do the letters ABV stand for?
9. Whisky that is not diluted before bottling is
labelled as what?
10. What does the additive E150a contribute to whisky?

Match the country with the wine.

1. Bitch
2. Red Nose Red
3. Blasted Church
4. Terre Arse
5. Cleavage Creek
6. Cat's Pee on a Gooseberry Bush
7. Sushi Wine
8. Oops
9. Marge 'n' Tina
10. The Unpronounceable Grape

a. Argentina
b. Australia
c. Canada
d. Chile
e. France
f. Hungary
g. Italy
h. New Zealand
i. South Africa
j. USA

COUNTRIES OF ORIGIN

PICK
A
YEAR

1. When was the first official classification of Bordeaux wine:
1815, 1855 or 1895?

2. When did America's four-year whiskey rebellion begin:
1771, 1791 or 1811?

3. When did the Royal Navy's daily ration of rum dry up:
1950, 1960 or 1970?

4. When was Robert Burns born:
1759, 1795 or 1815?

5. When was the first golden lager brewed:
1842, 1877 or 1891?

6. When was the launch of Wild Turkey bourbon:
1911, 1928 or 1940?

7. When was Munich's inaugural Oktoberfest:
1775, 1810 or 1848?

8. When was the first tax on Scottish whisky:
1644, 1759 or 1823?

9. When did Guinness first leave the shores of Ireland:
1686, 1769 or 1851?

10. When does the history of wine roughly begin:
8000 BC, 5000 BC or 3000 BC?

1. Which award-winning English beer is said to be Madonna's favourite?

2. How is the Volstead Act better known?

3. Mix whisky with oatmeal and honey and what do you have?

4. What type of wine is the French Tavel?

5. In a bottle of wine, the air gap between the cork and the alcohol is known as what?

6. The Italian liqueur Strega is what colour?

7. What was once known as the 'Englishman's Wine'?

8. What is the dominant grape variety in Chianti?

9. Indian whisky is often made from which non-Scotch ingredient?

10. What do Armagnac and the French musketeer d'Artagnan have in common?

MIXED
BATCH (1)

VIN

BLANC

1. The Chenin Blanc grape is most associated with French wines of which region?

2. Jurançon wine is made in the foothills of which mountain range?

3. Which popular white wine comes from around the city of Nantes in western France?

4. Is Pouilly-Fuissé a wine from Burgundy or the Loire?

5. Which one of these is not a French white wine: Barsac, Madiran, Vouvray?

6. What type of wine is Monbazillac from the Bergerac region?

7. The predominantly white wine region of Entre-Deux-Mers in Bordeaux is between which 'two seas'?

8. Which white wine from Alsace means 'spicy grape'?

9. What grape is used to make Sancerre?

10. Which champagne is drier, brut or sec?

---

1. Loire 2. Pyrenees (south-west France). 3. Muscadet. 4. Burgundy. 5. Madiran. 6. Sweet. 7. The rivers Garonne and Dordogne, so not seas at all. 8. Gewürztraminer (gewürz means spice, traminer is a variety of grape). 9. Sauvignon. 10. Brut. Although sec is French for dry, in the case of champagne it's only 'medium-dry'.

Put together the ingredients and what classic cocktails do you get?

1. Brandy and crème de menthe.
2. Champagne and freshly squeezed peach juice.
3. Gin, lemon juice, caster sugar, soda water.
4. Brandy, Cointreau, lemon juice.
5. Vodka, orange juice, Galliano.
6. Gin, Cointreau, lemon juice.
7. Brandy, gin, lemon juice, soda water.
8. Sweet vermouth, Campari, gin, citrus peel, soda water.
9. Dark rum, lime juice, syrup, soda water.
10. Tequila, lime juice, maraschino, grenadine, egg white.

COCKTAIL

MIX

REAL
ALES

Name the breweries behind these outstanding British beers.

1. Explorer.
2. Old Speckled Hen.
3. Bishop's Finger.
4. Gem.
5. Tiger Best Bitter.
6. Wandle Ale.
7. Nut Brown Ale.
8. Harvest Ale.
9. Old Tom.
10. Dark Ruby Mild.

1. What is the Shiraz grape called in France?
2. Which grape is used to make the French wine Chablis?
3. What is Spanish for vineyard?
4. The white Viognier grape is associated with which French wine region: Alsace, Loire or Rhône?
5. What is the only grape permitted in the production of red Beaujolais?
6. The Nebbiolo grape is native to which country?
7. What destroyed countless vineyards in France and elsewhere in the late 19th century?
8. Which one of these grapes is white: Colombard, Pinotage or Sangiovese?
9. How is the German Klingelberger grape better known?
10. What is a vieilles vignes?

10. ('Old vine') Wine made from vines that are at least 20 years old.

1. Syrah. 2. Chardonnay. 3. Viña. 4. Rhône. 5. Gamay. 6. Italy. 7. The phylloxera aphid. 8. Colombard. 9. Riesling.

ON THE GRAPEVINE

TRUE OR FALSE?

1. Vin de garage refers to wine made on a very small scale.

2. Only whiskey produced in the state of Kentucky can be legally described as bourbon.

3. St Drostan is the patron saint of whisky distillers.

4. Edward VII was the inspiration for a liqueur called The King's Ginger.

5. A Korean wine has dead mice as an essential ingredient.

6. Pom-pom was a 19th-century term for a brandy balloon.

7. Sparkling wine was not invented by Dom Pérignon.

8. In China, beer is sometimes sold in plastic bags.

9. A squeeze of toothpaste accompanied by hot water is the best way to clean a decanter.

10. William Teacher, founder of the Scotch whisky dynasty, was teetotal.

1. What is the fuel traditionally used to dry malted barley in the kiln?

2. Malt whisky is often matured in casks that have previously contained one or other of which two alcoholic drinks?

3. What is the padlocked glass-fronted box through which spirit passes as it leaves the still?

4. What did Aeneas Coffey invent in 1830?

5. The coiled copper tube along which vapours condense in a still is called a what?

6. What is grist?

7. Roughly what percentage of alcohol evaporates each year from a cask of maturing whisky?

8. What are 'foreshots' and 'feints'?

9. What name is given to the alcoholic liquid before it enters the distillation process?

10. Does whisky age in the bottle?

MAKING
SCOTCH

1. 'If you drink, don't drive. Don't even putt.'
a) Dave Allen, b) Dean Martin, c) Rich Hall

2. 'I'd rather have a bottle in front of me than a frontal lobotomy.'
a) Phyllis Diller, b) Kathy Lette, c) Dorothy Parker

3. 'Always do sober what you said you'd do drunk.
That will teach you to keep your mouth shut.'
a) Kingsley Amis, b) Ernest Hemingway, c) Will Self

4. 'I have taken more out of alcohol than alcohol
has taken out of me.'
a) Winston Churchill, b) Evelyn Waugh, c) Mae West

5. 'It provokes the desire, but it takes away the performance.'
a) Samuel Johnson, b) William Shakespeare, c) Oscar Wilde

6. 'Wine is bottled poetry.'
a) Francis Ford Coppola, b) David Lloyd George, c) Robert Louis Stevenson

7. 'Too much of anything is bad, but too much
Champagne is just right.'
a) Julia Child, b) Noël Coward, c) F Scott Fitzgerald

8. 'What contemptible scoundrel stole the cork from my lunch?'
a) Mel Brooks, b) WC Fields, c) Groucho Marx

9. 'Zen martini: A martini with no vermouth at all.
And no gin, either.'
a) Anthony Bourdain, b) Giles Coren, c) PJ O'Rourke

10. 'Beer is the cause and solution to all of life's problems.'
a) Jeremy Clarkson, b) Karl Marx, c) Homer Simpson

---

1. Dean Martin. **2.** Dorothy Parker. **3.** Ernest Hemingway. **4.** William Shakespeare (Macbeth). **5.** Winston Churchill. **6.** Robert Louis Stevenson. **7.** F Scott Fitzgerald. **8.** W C Fields. **9.** PJ O'Rourke. **10.** Homer Simpson.

1. Who introduced cider to Britain?

2. A cider house is called what in France?

3. What is the American name for apple brandy?

4. Which British perry launched in the 1950s was a sparkling success?

5. What is pomace?

6. What annual ritual takes place in West Country orchards to ensure a good harvest for the coming year?

7. What is the world's best-selling cider brand?

8. Which French liqueur is made from the William pear?

9. Prior to pressing, apple pulp is built into a stack called a what: cake, cheese or cob?

10. Which region of Spain is noted for its cider bars?

APPLES
AND
PEARS

VINO

ITALIANO

1. Which Italian wine is most associated with Tuscany?
2. Which popular wine manages to be both red and sparkling?
3. Sicily is the home of which fortified wine?
4. The red wines Barola and Barbaresco come from which region of Italy?
5. Which grape is used to make sparkling Asti?
6. Production of which familiar white wine is centred around Rome?
7. What is the Italian equivalent of appellation contrôlée (initials will do)?
8. Pinot Grigio is the Italian name for what?
9. Soave white wine is produced in which region: Emilia-Romagna, Lombardy or Veneto?
10. Which Italian grape produces a red wine very similar in style to Californian Zinfandel?

1. Chianti. 2. Lambrusco. 3. Marsala. 4. Piedmont. 5. Moscato Bianco. 6. Frascati. 7. DOC (Denominazione di Origine Controllata). 8. Pinot Gris. 9. Veneto. 10. Primitivo.

1. Which liqueur shares its name with a biscuit?

2. In The Archers, which brand of beer is served in The Bull?

3. Malmsey and Sercial are varieties of which wine?

4. The Russian brew Kvass is made from fermented what?

5. What was Falstaff's favourite tipple?

6. For which beer is Rutland famous?

7. Suhindol is a wine from which country?

8. Malt whisky stills are traditionally made of what?

9. What name is given to the film of yeast that forms on the surface of certain wines, dictating their style?

10. Which Italian vermouth's name means 'one and a half points'?

MIXED
BATCH (2)

COMING
TO TERMS
WITH BEER

1. What is the stopper in the hole of a barrel called?

2. The word lager is derived from the German for what?

3. Lambic beers are native to which country?

4. What do the initials IPA on a label stand for?

5. Why was milk stout so called?

6. When was the Campaign for Real Ale (CAMRA) founded: 1951, 1961 or 1971?

7. Which popular 19th-century beer was halfway between a bitter and a stout?

8. What is a butt?

9. An IBU measures what in beer?

10. What is combined with beer to make a 'Snakebite'?

1. Which Scotch whisky is branded with a striding man?
2. Which Scottish town calls itself the
'Whisky Capital of the World'?
3. On which Scottish island is the Talisker distillery?
4. In which English county is the St George's Distillery?
5. What is Scotland's smallest distillery?
6. Which whisky brand was named after a
ship built on the River Clyde?
7. What is Scotland's northernmost distillery?
8. What is the Hebridean island of Mull's sole distillery?
9. Which whisky brand encouraged consumers
not to be vague?
10. What heady distinction does the Braeval Distillery
in Banffshire have?

1. Johnnie Walker. Illustrator Tom Browne created the Striding Man logo in 1908. 2. Dufftown (Morayshire).
3. Skye. 4. Norfolk (The English Whisky Co) 5. Edradour. 6. Cutty Sark. 7. Highland Park on the Isle of Orkney.
8. Tobermory. 9. Haig with its slogan 'Don't be vague – Ask for Haig'. 10. It is Scotland's highest distillery.

ON THE

WHISKY

TRAIL

FICTIONAL
WATERING
HOLES

1. What is Del Boy's local in *Only Fools and Horses*?

2. In which convivial watering hole is Bertie Wooster often to be found?

3. What was The Bull's sole competitor in Ambridge until it was converted into apartments?

4. In *The Hitchhiker's Guide to the Galaxy*, where do Arthur Dent and Ford Prefect go for a drink before the world ends?

5. What is the name of the establishment owned by Rick Blaine in *Casablanca*?

6. In *Men Behaving Badly*, Gary and Tony regularly misbehave in which pub?

7. Who historically finds peace of mind at the Potwell Inn?

8. The inimitable Arthur Daly is a long-standing member of which drinking club?

9. Which Boston bar competitively rivals *Cheers*?

10. In which Charles Dickens novel is there a tavern called The Six Jolly Fellowship Porters?

---

1. The Nag's Head. 2. The Drones Club. 3. The Cat and Fiddle (The Archers). 4. The Horse and Groom. 5. Rick's Café Américain. 6. The Crown. 7. Mr Polly (The History of Mr Polly). 8. The Winchester Club (Minder). 9. Gary's Old Towne Tavern. 10. *Our Mutual Friend*.

1. What does the Russian word vodka mean?

2. The 1808 Rum Rebellion took place in which British colony?

3. Which popular spirit is made from the fermented juice of the blue agave plant?

4. Produced on the Isle of Man, ManX is a clear spirit distilled from what?

5. What fruit is at the heart of Slivovitz?

6. Which Greek spirit is a blend of brandy, spices and wine?

7. Xellent vodka is a product of which country: Iceland, New Zealand or Switzerland?

8. Which spirit was traditionally drunk with the aid of a spoon and a sugar cube?

9. What do you get when you mix white rum with lime juice?

10. Which anise-flavoured spirit is widely drunk in the Middle East?

GETTING INTO INTO THE SPIRITS

SONGS FOR SWINGING DRINKERS

Fill in the drink-related missing words of these song titles.

1. 'Naked Women And . . .'
2. 'The Piano Has Been . . .'
3. '. . . In The Closet'
4. 'Straight . . . Night'
5. 'Spill The . . .'
6. 'The . . . Let Me Down'
7. 'Hooray For . . .'
8. 'Two . . . Away'
9. 'Streams Of . . .'
10. 'Pass The . . .'

1. What do the French call a wine cellar?
2. Which country is the bigger wine producer, Italy or Spain?
3. Ygrec is a dry white offshoot of which legendary French wine?
4. What is the world's most easterly wine region?
5. How many of the USA's 50 states are wine producers?
6. Mousseux is wine of what type?
7. The award-winning wine Ballet of Angels is made in which US state: Connecticut, New Mexico or Wyoming?
8. What is added to the Greek wine Retsina to produce its distinctive flavour?
9. Vin jaune is a speciality of which region of France?
10. What is the English term for wine from the Rhine?

1. Cave. 2. Italy. 3. Château d'Yquem. 4. Gisborne, New Zealand. 5. All 50. 6. Sparkling. 7. Connecticut. 8. Pine resin. 9. Jura. The 'yellow wine' is matured in casks for six years under a film of yeast, which gives it its characteristic flavour. 10. Hock.

ODD
BINS

NAME THAT BEER

Match the beer with the slogan.

1. It's What Your Right Arm's For.
2. Good Things Come To Those Who Wait.
3. The Beer The Men Drink.
4. The Champagne Of Beers.
5. It Looks Good, It Tastes Good,
And By Golly It Does You Good.
6. Reassuringly Expensive.
7. It's A Bit Gorgeous.
8. It Works Every Time.
9. The Other Side Of Dark.
10. If I Wanted Water, I Would Have Asked For Water.

1. What nationality was the pioneer Irish distiller John Jameson?

2. How many times is Irish whiskey normally distilled?

3. Which Irish Republican leader has a whiskey in his name?

4. Irish pot still whiskey is made from which combination of cereals?

5. Which one of the four existing Irish distilleries is in Northern Ireland?

6. Which legendary Russian tsar was a fan of Irish whiskey?

7. The Old Jameson Distillery in Dublin was a location for which John le Carré spy film?

8. Which major brand was named after the company's most successful salesman?

9. What is a 'ball of malt'?

10. Which famous Irish writer had the Jameson logo imprinted on his wallet?

DROP OF
THE IRISH

SIZE
MATTERS

1. A magnum holds how many litres?

2. Which cask is larger, a firkin or kilderkin?

3. What is the term for a cask of port?

4. How much does a noggin measure?

5. Which biblical king's name has come to mean a bottle containing 15 litres?

6. What is a 'growler'?

7. Which country serves the smallest shots: Germany, Italy or the UK?

8. What is the measuring device attached to bottles in a bar called?

9. Which jeroboam holds more, Bordeaux or Burgundy?

10. Which former Australian prime minister held the world record for the fastest downing of a yard of ale?

1. In which direction should port travel around the table?

2. What was Margaret Thatcher's favourite brand of whisky?

3. Where in London is the Meantime brewery?

4. The 19th-century journalist Alfred Barnard wrote a classic book about which alcoholic beverage?

5. Fortnum & Mason's English sparkling wine is a product of which county?

6. Madeira is Portuguese for what?

7. What is the principal ingredient in Irish Mist liqueur, apart from whiskey?

8. Which wine producer insists on having the Director's Cut?

9. What is a Basquaise?

10. Which Portuguese wine can be red or white but never green?

MIXED
BATCH (3)

WINES OF THE
NEW WORLD

1. Which grape native to south-west France has become most identified with Argentina?

2. Where is known as the 'Chardonnay Capital of New Zealand'?

3. Which New World country produces the most wine?

4. In which Australian state is the highly regarded Pipers Brook vineyard?

5. Which wine region in Chile is best known for its Cabernet Sauvignon?

6. Which is South Africa's oldest wine region: Constantia, Paarl or Stellenbosch?

7. In which US state is the Volcano Winery?

8. Which one of these is not an Australian wine region: Grampians, Pyrenees, Snowy Valley?

9. Under the Table is a red wine from which country?

10. In 2010, which government declared the country's wines to be its national drink?

Supply the missing word for each of these distinctively named British pubs.

1. The . . . Bedstead
2. Bull and . . .
3. Ye Olde Trip to . . .
4. The Fox Goes . . .
5. The . . . Dog
6. The Eagle and . . .
7. Larwood and . . .
8. The Cat and . . . Pot
9. The Atmospheric . . . Inn
10. The . . . Taxpayer

9. Railway. 10. Jolly.

1. Flying. 2. Mouth. 3. Jerusalem. 4. Free. 5. Guide. 6. Child. 7. Voce (famous Notts cricketers). 8. Custard.

PUZZLING

PUBS

COMING TO TERMS WITH WINE

1. What does premier cru mean?

2. Wine made stronger by the addition of brandy is called what?

3. The trails that flow down the side of a glass after the wine has been swirled around are its what?

4. Which type of wine is made from grapes that have frozen on the vine?

5. The word côte often features on a French wine label – what does it mean?

6. What word describes wine made from, and named after, a single or dominant grape variety?

7. How is an itinerant airborne viniculturist more commonly known?

8. What is vin gris?

9. What is the unfermented mix of grape juice, pulp, pips and skins called?

10. The parasitic fungus that is used to enhance the quality of certain sweet wines is known as what?

---

1. First growth. 2. Fortified wine. 3. Legs. 4. Icewine or (in Germany) Eiswein. 5. Slope or hillside (as in Côtes du Rhône). 6. Varietal. 7. Flying winemaker. 8. A type of very pale rosé. 9. Must. 10. Noble rot (Botrytis cinerea).

1. What is the very first drink ordered by James Bond in *Casino Royale*, the first 007 novel?

2. What is Bridget Jones's favourite wine?

3. In which dystopian novel will you find Victory Gin?

4. Which New York girl-about-town's preferred tipple is 'one-half vodka, one-half gin, no vermouth'?

5. In *A Christmas Carol*, Scrooge promises to share a bowl of Smoking Bishop with Bob Cratchit. What is Smoking Bishop?

6. Who invented the Pan Galactic Gargle Blaster?

7. Which Raymond Chandler novel made the Gin Gimlet a fashionable cocktail in the USA?

8. In a 1947 novel by Compton Mackenzie, what gets washed ashore on a remote Scottish island?

9. In F Scott Fitzgerald's *The Great Gatsby*, what do the protagonists drink in New York's Plaza Hotel?

10. Whose hangover cure, comprising Worcester Sauce, raw egg and red pepper, lands him the job?

---

1. An Americano. **2.** Chardonnay. **3.** *Nineteen Eighty-Four* by George Orwell. **4.** Holly Golightly's, in Truman Capote's Breakfast at Tiffany's. **5.** A mulled punch, made with port, red wine, oranges and spices. **6.** Zaphod Beeblebrox, in The Hitchhiker's Guide to the Galaxy by Douglas Adams. **7.** *The Long Goodbye*. **8.** A ship's cargo of whisky (*Whisky Galore*). **9.** Mint Juleps. **10.** Jeeves's. He is interviewed for the job of manservant by a seriously hungover Bertie Wooster (Jeeves Takes Charge).

LITERARY
TIPPLES

DRINK GOOD
ENOUGH TO EAT

1. Which alcohol is a traditional ingredient in cheesecake?

2. A Tipsy Orange is best made with a splash of which Scottish liqueur?

3. Which two alcoholic beverages go into poulet à la Normande?

4. What is the Alsace version of coq au vin?

5. Which local brew is added to the oriental hotpot nabemono?

6. Carbonnade à la Flamande would not be complete without which national beer?

7. Which wine fortifies a Sicilian cassata cake?

8. The Swiss often use which liqueur to boost a cheese fondue?

9. What helps to turn cheese on toast into something more rare?

10. Which steak dish is flambéed in brandy before being served?

---

9. Beer (Welsh Rarebit). 10. Steak Diane.

1. Bourbon. 2. Drambuie. 3. Calvados and cider. 4. Coq au Riesling. 5. Saké. 6. Belgian. 7. Marsala. 8. Kirsch.

1. What is the definition of a single malt whisky?

2. Which Scottish whisky region boasts the most distilleries?

3. Which single malt shares the name of a famous sea battle?

4. Milford Single Malt is produced in which country?

5. Which single malt is nicknamed the 'Manzanilla of the North'?

6. George Smith was the legendary founder of which Scottish distillery?

7. What is the world's best-selling single malt?

8. Which well-known single malt comes from the Scottish town of Tain?

9. In which country is Murree Single Malt made?

10. Which single malt claimed consumers would either 'love it or hate it'?

9. Pakistan. 10. Laphroaig.
some of the coastal influences of the Spanish sherry). 6. The Glenlivet. 7. Glenfiddich. 8. Glenmorangie.
1. A malt whisky from a single distillery. 2. Speyside. 3. Scapa. 4. New Zealand. 5. Old Pulteney (because it shares

SINGULAR

MALTS

MOTHER'S RUIN

1. What is the principal botanical element used to flavour gin?

2. Pink Gin is traditionally made with which type of gin?

3. Gin originated in which country?

4. In the British colonies gin was used to mask the bitter flavour of which medicinal compound?

5. What style of gin was the sweeter forerunner of 'London Dry'?

6. Which nation consumes the most gin?

7. In the Prohibition era, what name was given to the domestically produced version of the spirit?

8. Where in the UK is the oldest working gin distillery?

9. Which gin hit the streets of London first, Gilbey's or Gordon's?

10. What fruit juice goes with gin to make a Gimlet?

1. Juniper berry. 2. Plymouth gin. 3. Holland, in the 17th century. 4. Quinine. 5. Old Tom Gin, which had petered out by the start of the 20th century. 6. The Philippines. 7. Bathtub gin, though it was seldom made in one. 8. Plymouth (Black Friars Distillery, home to Plymouth Gin, founded 1793). 9. Gordon's (Alexander Gordon opened a distillery in London in 1769). 10. Lime juice.

In which countries are these wine regions located?

1. Casablanca Valley
2. Barsac
3. Gippsland
4. Uco Valley
5. Ahr
6. Walla Walla Valley
7. Elgin
8. Bierzo
9. Fraser Valley
10. Dealu Mare

WHERE IN THE WORLD?

SHAKEN AND
STIRRED

1. What puts the kick in a Moscow Mule?

2. Where is home to the Mojito?

3. Which type of whiskey was used in the original Manhattan?

4. Which vodka-based cocktail has a DIY ring to it?

5. What is mixed with whisky to make a Rusty Nail?

6. Pernod, grenadine and soda are the genetic make-up of which colourful animal?

7. Where does the Pisco in a Pisco Sour come from?

8. Which B&B has nothing to do with bed and breakfast?

9. US comedian George Jessel is credited with creating which classic cocktail?

10. Whether it's beer chasing whisky or the other way round, what is it?

1. Vodka. 2. Cuba. 3. Rye. 4. Screwdriver. 5. Drambuie. 6. Pink Panther. 7. Chile or Peru. 8. Brandy and Bénédictine (aka B&B). 9. Bloody Mary. 10. A Boilermaker.

1. What is James Bond's bubbly brand of choice?

2. Which influential writer on beer and whisky died in 2007?

3. What is the actual gem behind Bombay Sapphire gin?

4. What is the single biggest wine-producing region in the world?

5. Whose bitter did Jack Dee promote on TV?

6. Curdle hot milk with wine or ale, spice it up and you have what old-fashioned comforting drink?

7. Who, in 1800, ordered 500 casks of Marsala wine as a pick-me-up for his fleet?

8. Which country is home to Van Der Hum liqueur?

9. Which Hollywood star is said to have once bathed in 350 bottles of champagne?

10. The label for Black & White whisky features two dogs of different breeds – what breeds?

MIXED
BATCH (4)

1. What is Spain's most common native red grape?

2. What is a bodega?

3. Rueda is best known for red or white wine?

4. Which type of sherry is made around the port of Sanlúcar de Barrameda?

5. The production of which Spanish wine is centred in the Penedès region of Catalonia?

6. Sherry is best drunk from which style of glass?

7. Which wine takes its name from the Andalucian city from which it originates?

8. What is the top category of Spanish wine, as indicated on the label?

9. Which major wine region spans the Ebro river?

10. Galicia in north-west Spain is renowned for white wines made from which grape?

9. Rioja. 10. Albariño.

1. Tempranillo. 2. Winery 3. White. 4. Manzanilla. 5. Cava. 6. A copita. 7. Malaga. 8. Gran Reserva.

1. What wine did Hannibal Lector elect to drink with human liver and fava beans?
2. Which malt whisky does James Bond favour in *Skyfall*?
3. Which grape comes out on top in the wine-tasting movie *Sideways*?
4. What bootleg booze is poured from a hot water bottle in *Some Like It Hot*?
5. Which cocktail does Cary Grant order over dinner on the train in *North By Northwest*?
6. The drink '7 and 7' is featured in the movie *Saturday Night Fever* – what does it comprise?
7. What is The Dude's favourite tipple in *The Big Lebowski*?
8. In the movie *Cocktail*, Tom Cruise mixes a Red Eye – what are its four ingredients?
9. What alcoholic beverage must be ice cold in *Alexandria*?
10. Which drink makes a fleeting appearance in the movie *Dorian Gray* whilst the eponymous hero is having his portrait painted?

DRINKING AT THE MOVIES

BEERS
AROUND
THE WORLD

1. Which US beer called itself the 'King of Beers'?

2. Heineken was first brewed in which country?

3. Which Australian beer took its name from the river on which Perth stands?

4. Scotland's Black Isle Brewery only makes what type of beer?

5. Kölsch is a speciality beer brewed in which German city?

6. Mac's Sassy Red is an award-winning amber ale in which former dominion?

7. Which beer claims to have made Milwaukee famous?

8. Chang is Thailand's No 1 beer – what does chang mean?

9. Einstök White Ale is a product of which European country?

10. The Belgian beer Chimay is made by which otherwise committed group of brewers?

1. Budweiser. 2. Netherlands. 3. Swan. 4. Organic. 5. Cologne. 6. New Zealand. 7. Schlitz. 8. Elephant. 9. Iceland (brewed 60 miles from the Arctic Circle). 10. Trappist monks.

1. Which member of the Hollywood Rat Pack did Bob Hope once describe as a 'test pilot for Seagram'?

2. Who was the first British TV chef to take a regular slurp whilst cooking?

3. Which American writer was famously partial to a Mojito cocktail?

4. Who found claret to be the perfect lubricant when commentating on cricket?

5. Which US Civil War general was noted for his penchant for whiskey?

6. Which vintage Hollywood tough guy said, 'I should never have switched from scotch to martinis'?

7. According to the gossip columns, Jennifer Aniston is attached to which classic cocktail?

8. A heady mix of Dubonnet and gin was whose right royal tipple?

9. Napoleon Bonaparte insisted on taking which great Burgundy on his military campaigns?

10. Who was buried with a song in his heart and a bottle of Jack Daniels in his coffin?

FAMOUS

TIPPLERS

WHISKY AND WHISKEY

1. Which Scottish island hosts an annual
Festival of Music and Malt?

2. The Chivas brothers, James and John, first started blending
their whisky in which Scottish city?

3. What type of American whiskey was the most popular
prior to Prohibition?

4. What 'old number' features on the Jack Daniels label?

5. Illicitly distilled whiskey is called what in America?

6. Which Scottish distillery has a statue commemorating
a feline 'employee'?

7. Whisky is best drunk out of which shape of glass?

8. Which US president distilled his own whiskey?

9. Where is the only grain whisky distillery in the
Scottish highlands?

10. What is the principal grain used to make bourbon?

1. Which Parisian bar did Ernest Hemingway liberate in August 1944?

2. Which London pub saw the start of the Salvation Army and witnessed a killing by one of the Kray twins?

3. In which New York bar did Welsh poet Dylan Thomas fatally down 18 shots of whiskey?

4. Which hotel bar gave birth to Singapore's signature cocktail, the Singapore Sling?

5. Which iconic Dublin bar is known as the 'home of the pint' [of Guinness]?

6. Where is the drinking establishment known as 'Ollie's Last Pub' (after its most celebrated customer, the actor Oliver Reed)?

7. Which bar in Venice was made a national landmark in 2001?

8. Which legendary New York 'Irish' bar was forced to admit women in 1970 after a court action was brought against it?

9. Actor Sir Ian McKellan became landlord of which historic pub in London's East End in 2011?

10. Which Glaswegian pub was the setting for Billy Connolly's 'The Last Supper' sketch?

1. The bar of the Ritz Hotel. 2. The Blind Beggar, Whitechapel Road. William Booth preached his first sermon outside and Ronnie Kray shot rival gangster George Cornell there. 3. White Horse Tavern. 4. Long Bar (Raffles Hotel). 5. Mulligans. 6. Valetta, Malta. Officially named The Pub, it is where Oliver Reed spent his last night alive in 1999. 7. Harry's Bar. 8. McSorley's Old Ale House. 9. The Grapes (Charles Dickens was allegedly a customer). 10. The Saracen's Head.

STAR

BARS

APRÈS REPAS

1. What do the initials VSOP on a bottle of cognac stand for?

2. Which Chartreuse is stronger, green or yellow?

3. How do the French prefer to drink port?

4. What is the Basque drink Patxaran made from?

5. Which liqueur is flavoured with caraway seed, cumin and fennel?

6. The word brandy comes from the Dutch brandewijn, meaning what?

7. Nocino is an Italian liqueur made from which nut: almond, hazelnut or walnut?

8. Grappa is a distillation of what?

9. What is the French equivalent of grappa?

10. At which English football club is Bénédictine always the drink of the day?

1. Very Superior (or Special) Old Pale. An indication that the youngest brandy in the blend has aged for at least four years. 2. Green. 3. As an aperitif. 4. Sloes. 5. Kümmel (pronounced 'küm-mel'). 6. Burnt wine. 7. Walnut. 8. The leftover grape pulp from the final wine pressing. 9. Marc (the 'c' is silent). 10. Burnley. A taste acquired in France by the East Lancashire Regiment during the First World War, the liqueur is a popular drink for supporters on match days.

1. Cloudy Bay comes from which New Zealand wine region?

2. What type of wine is the legendary Château d'Yquem?

3. Which great Bordeaux wine does Samuel Pepys
refer to in his diary as 'Ho Bryan'?

4. Is the classic white Puligny-Montrachet from
Burgundy or the Loire?

5. Screaming Eagle is one of which country's
most sought-after Cabernets?

6. Is the famous Château Pétrus a Margaux,
Pomerol or St Emilion?

7. Which French red wine is noted for the 17th-century
tower that stands amongst its vines?

8. Vega Sicilia Unico is one of which country's
most expensive wines?

9. Where in Australia is Penfold's flagship
wine Grange produced?

10. Which home to a Burgundy grand cru is often
abbreviated to DRC?

1. Marlborough. 2. Sauternes. 3. Haut Brion (10 April 1663). 4. Burgundy. 5. USA (California). 6. Pomerol.
7. Château Latour. 8. Spain's. 9. Barossa Valley. 10. Domaine de la Romanée-Conti. Many consider Romanée-Conti
the finest of all Burgundy reds.

NAME DROPPING
WINES

WHOSE
QUAFFABLE
QUOTES?

1. 'Claret is the liquor for boys; port for men; but he who aspires to be a hero must drink brandy.'

a) Rudyard Kipling, b) Samuel Johnson, c) George Orwell

2. 'There is no bad whiskey. There are only some whiskeys that aren't as good as others.'

a) Raymond Chandler, b) Ernest Hemingway, c) Hunter S Thompson

3. 'Here's a bottle and an honest friend!'

a) Robert Burns, b) Charles Dickens, c) William Shakespeare

4. 'An alcoholic is someone who drinks more than their doctor.'

a) Barry Cryer, b) Eddie Izzard, c) Robin Williams

5. 'I'm a Method actor. I spent years training for the drinking and carousing I had to do in this film.'

a) George Clooney, b) Robert De Niro, c) Mickey Rourke

6. 'Scotch whisky to a Scotchman is as innocent as milk is to the rest of the human race.'

a) Bill Bryson, b) Mark Twain, c) PG Wodehouse

7. 'You're not drunk if you can lie on the floor without holding on.'

a) Peter Cook, b) Kathy Lette, c) Dean Martin

8. 'I never drink anything stronger than gin before breakfast.'

a) WC Fields, b) George Melly, c) William Shatner

9. 'Not one man in a beer commercial has a beer belly.'

a) Roseanne Barr, b) Jay Leno, c) Rita Rudner

10. 'The three-martini lunch is the epitome of American efficiency. Where else can you get an earful, a bellyful and a snootful at the same time?'

a) George H Bush, b) Gerald Ford, c) Harry Truman

---

1. Samuel Johnson. 2. Raymond Chandler. 3. Robert Burns. 4. Barry Cryer. 5. George Clooney. 6. Mark Twain. 7. Dean Martin. 8. W C Fields. 9. Rita Rudner. 10. Gerald Ford.

1. What is the name of the Royle family's local?
2. What is unusual about the Penderyn distillery, home of the Welsh Whisky Company?
3. Which cocktail comprising five parts chocolate liqueur and one part bourbon is named after an iconic British rock singer?
4. What is the German term for sparkling wine?
5. What is Carlsberg when it's not a beer?
6. What pre-prandial tipple ceased to be 'British' in 1996?
7. What do the award-winning initials CBOB stand for?
8. 'Barbed wire' is Australian slang for which beer?
9. Which silly ass is said to have inadvertently unearthed the benefits of pruning vines?
10. Work, according to Oscar Wilde, is the curse of what?

1. The Feathers. 2. It also distils vodka and gin. 3. The David Bowie. 4. Sekt. 5. A Czech herbal liqueur. 6. British Sherry. Under new legislation only wine produced in the Jerez region of Spain could be branded sherry. 7. Champion Beer Of Britain (awarded annually by CAMRA). 8. Castlemaine XXXX. 9. Bishop Martin (afterwards St Martin) of Tours' donkey. It tucked into some vines that later, to everyone's amazement, grew back more profusely. 10. The drinking classes.

MIXED

BATCH (5)

ABOUT THE AUTHOR

Graham Tarrant has written books on a variety of subjects and is the editor of several anthologies, along with other works about food and drink. His companion quiz book for foodies, *Everything But the Oink,* is also published by Absolute Press.

He lives in Wiltshire and in the Pays Basque, with the vineyards of Bordeaux, Navarra and Rioja reassuringly within reach.